Living What We Say We Believe

S T U D E N T   J O U R N A L

Contents

Accelerated Spiritual Growth
for Individuals and Families

Written by Randy Petersen, Jim Hancock, and Mitch Vander Vorst

Editor: Mitch Vander Vorst
Cover Illustration: Thomason Design Center
Cover & Text Design: De Leon Design

The passion of Mainstay Church Resources is to facilitate revival among God's people by helping pastors help people develop healthy spiritual habits in nine vital areas that always characterize genuine times of awakening. To support this goal, Mainstay Church Resources uses a C.H.U.R.C.H. strategy to provide practical tools and resources, including the annual 50-Day Spiritual Adventure, the Seasonal Advent Celebration, the 4-Week Festival of Worship, and the Pastor's Toolbox.

Printed in the United States of America

Helping Pastors
Help People Grow

ISBN 1-57849-107-X

It's hard to find anything real in our world anymore. Politics is all spin. Entertainment is all hype. Sports is all about shoe endorsements.

Take music (please!). A few years ago, everyone went bonkers over any garage band anywhere close to Seattle. This was "authentic," "genuine," the heartfelt cries of a new generation. Suddenly the alternative sound was hot, and the grunge look was in. You probably went out and bought a flannel shirt and tore holes in your jeans—all in order to look "authentic." In the years since, alternative has become mainstream. Musicians work really hard to sound "genuine."

Are you getting the irony in all this? What happened to just plain reality? Maybe it's different when you get closer to home. Do you find reality at school, in your family, among your friends? Maybe some, but you know how it is. There are kids who play politics with the teachers and everyone else. Even here, it's all based on appearances. You smile at your parents like a good kid but grumble when they're gone. Even dating can become a sense-less game, as you pretend to be smarter, funnier, and more attractive than you are, yet hoping that someone will love you for who you "really" are. What's wrong with this picture?

Will you dare to be real? You can stop playing the games. Get honest with God, with yourself, with your family, with your friends. Make good promises and keep them. Face up to your faults and try to do better (and not just at covering them up).

That's what this Adventure is about. Over the next 50 days, this journal will coach you in ways to open up your real self. There will be prayers to pray, passages of the Bible to study, friends to connect with, activities to try. It'll be scary sometimes, exciting at times, maybe a bit boring on occasion. But everything here is designed to help you cut through the spin and hype and be who you are before God and others.

Obviously, you've got to make the Adventure your own. Don't do this to please your folks or to score points with your youth leader. Do it because you're tired of playing games and you want to get serious about following Jesus.

So, can you take a chance on being the real deal? Can you live what you say you believe? Take a deep breath and let's get started. Here we go. . . .

• **Pray** that God will help you realize what you really believe and value. Ask him what "reality checks" he'd like to see you resolve through this Adventure.

• **Commit** yourself to this Adventure. Take it seriously. If you give it some time and attention, you'll be rolling in the payoff. Check it out for a few days and then try to get solid before the first week is over.

• **Get real.** Be honest with yourself, and with God, as you answer the questions in this journal. Use codes if you're afraid of a snoop. And when it comes time, at the end of each week, to decide whether or not you want to sign your name next to a promise, put some real thought into it. Make it a real promise.

• **Relax.** If you miss a day, don't go crazy trying to make it up. Just get going on the current day. Later, go back and see what you missed.

• **Connect** with others. Try doing this Adventure with a few friends or your youth group. You can keep tabs on each other and pool new ideas and support. (This is also an important part of Action Step 2.)

• **Prepare** yourself by taking a look at the journal now, especially pages 5–11. During the Adventure, you'll take five action steps. Some may be fairly basic and familiar; others involve more prep. But don't worry! Every week the Backcheck/Coming Attractions pages will keep you on track.

The top of each daily page has a place for the date. Take a second to locate a calendar. Find the Sunday you plan to begin the Adventure. Write that date in the blank on Sunday, Day 1. Then write the dates, in order, on all the pages that follow.

• **Expect to grow.** Great things can happen to you as you do this Adventure. God moves in powerful ways when people let him work through them. He can make a big difference in your life, too.

• **Ask questions.** Don't expect to get all the info on your own. There may be some things that you just don't get. At the bottom of each daily page there is a space to write down your unanswered questions—what you don't know, don't understand, or just don't get. Don't write these down and toss them. Try to get them answered—do some research on your own, ask someone who might be able to help, or talk about these questions in your youth group or at church.

O ver the next 50 days, this journal will focus on eight "reality checks" and five action steps that challenge you to begin thinking about what you really believe and value and how that affects your everyday life. At the end of each reality check you will be asked to consider a promise—to yourself, to God, and to those you care about—to make your own. If you're not ready to promise, think about it some more and come back to it when you're ready. You'll have other chances to reconsider throughout the journal.

THE REALITY CHECKS	THE PROMISES
1. Get Deep with God (p. 13)	*Spend some time each day with God.*
2. Get Real with Each Other (p. 22)	*Be honest and make friendships really count.*
3. Get Some Help with the Hard Stuff (p. 31)	*Practice living a life that pleases God.*
4. Get Right with Your Family (p. 40)	*Make family relationships a priority.*
5. Get Pumped About God's Work (p. 49)	*Appreciate and support the work of my church.*
6. Get Over the Walls (p. 58)	*Identify and deal with my prejudices.*
7. Get a Job (p. 67)	*Join God in his work in this world.*
8. Get a Life (p. 75)	*Live my life one day at a time through the power of Christ.*

Every Day
- **Read** the assigned Bible passages and answer the questions in the journal.
- **Breathe deep the breath of God** by taking few deep breaths and praying the Real Deal Prayer: "What do you want to do today, Jesus?" (Action Step 1, p. 6).
- **Care for those who care for you** through acts of kindness (Action Step 4, p. 9).

Every Week
- **Team up** with other Christians and get real with each other (Action Step 2, p. 7).
- **Throw down your signature sin** by following the six steps that will help you defeat it (Action Step 3, p. 8).

ONCE
- **Start climbing the walls** by starting a relationship with someone who has a different story from yours (Action Step 5, p. 10).

BONUS
- **Memorize** Bible passages that help you live what you say you believe. Consider using The Real Deal Scripture Pack to keep some important Bible passages with you throughout the day (see p. 15).

For a complete description of the action steps, see pages 6–10.

Breathe Deep the Breath of God

Every Day

Some locker rooms ought to have biohazard warning signs, don't you think? Put enough sweat-sogged shirts and socks in an enclosed space, and the air gets a bit thick. You don't even want to think about the new life-forms that could be breeding there. Getting a solid whiff of some lockers could send you into a coma.

Until we step into such an atmospherically challenged environment, we tend to take breathing for granted. We don't even think about it. You've taken about 5 million breaths in the past year, and you've probably forgotten most of them.

In the original languages of the Bible, the word for *Spirit* is the same as the word for *breath*. God's Spirit is a wind blowing all around us but also a breath blowing through us—filling us, getting us through the day.

What if your relationship with God became as natural as breathing? What if you started each day inhaling his presence and kept it going through the day? "How are you doing, Lord? How am I doing? Thanks for what happened just then. I'm going to need some major help next period." If that kind of "breathing" was your reality, it would change your life.

It's the real deal, and it starts with that first, deep breath.

Getting It Done:

The Real Deal Prayer: *"What do you want to do today, Jesus?"* Every morning, take at least 30 seconds to "breathe deep the breath of God." Take a few actual breaths and pray, "What do you want to do today, Jesus?" That's the prayer for this Adventure. And remember, it's not just a rhetorical question. Jesus may answer by asking you to spend some additional time in prayer, talk to that guy who always sits alone in the back of the bus, apologize to your sister for last night's fight, or memorize a certain passage of the Bible. It could be Jesus' answer doesn't seem that "spiritual" to you. Maybe he'll ask you to be quiet and rest or call your best friend or wash the dog. Who knows what the answer might be. The important thing is to listen.

Then, as you find a few moments throughout the day, repeat the process. A few deep breaths and: "What do you want to do today, Jesus?" You will find the more you pray this prayer, listen for Jesus' answer, and follow his lead, the closer you will be to God throughout each day.

In order to get deep with God, you will need to spend time with him. This prayer is one way to do that. Another way you will be breathing deep the breath of God is by reading Bible passages each day and taking time to answer the questions in this journal. You may also find it helpful to carry some of God's breath with you—in your pocket or in your head. That's what The Real Deal Scripture Pack is for (see p. 15). You can carry Adventure Bible verses with you wherever you go. And the pack is a great tool to help you memorize some of God's Word—then you really will be able to breathe deep the breath of God.

Team Up

Every Week

If you're into sports, you've got to love teamwork. The highlight film may show that spectacular slam, but the last TV shots of the Final Four show the winning team jumping up and down—together. Teamwork: It works.

We need to team up as Christians, too. A huge hunk of the Bible is *about* teamwork, and yet we often prefer to go it alone. We don't ask others about their relationship with God, and we don't want to be asked. We'll talk about college basketball or Leo DiCaprio but not about Christ.

What's that all about? It's time to team up. Grab a friend or three and agree to help one another be better Christians. Start talking about what's most important to you.

Getting It Done:

Find one Christian friend (or maybe two or three), and ask them to check up on you each week of the Adventure. All that's necessary is to ask how you're doing on these action steps, but you could make it an even stronger checkup if you want (see below). Of course, if the others are also doing the Adventure, you could check up on one another.

Getting Real with Each Other

Sometimes we avoid talking about what we believe and who we really are with others because we're not sure what to say or what they will say. The truth is, everyone is searching for some reality, someone to share their true self with—weaknesses and all. These questions can help you get past the surface and into the real:
• How have you felt God working in your life today?
• When is it toughest for you to be a Christian?
• Do you think you're a stronger Christian now than you were a year ago? Why?
• What changes do you think God wants to make in your life over the next few months?
• How do you think your relationship with God will be different 10 years from now?
• Read any good Scripture lately?
• What have you learned at church (Sunday school, youth group) lately?
• Has God ever totally surprised you?
• If God would answer only one question for you, what would you ask?
• What have you been praying for lately?

Tips for Teaming Up
• Be honest. This is not a "spiritual" act. If you're having trouble, say so.
• If you feel threatened, it's fair to say, "I'd rather not talk about that."
• If you're asking the questions, don't pry. Allow for some privacy.
• You're going to goof up sometimes in your Christian life, maybe even during this Adventure. Don't get paralyzed by guilt. Be honest about it.
• When others on your team goof up, remind them of the forgiveness of Christ and gently challenge them to get back on the right road.

Throw Down Your Signature Sin

Every Week (Starting in Week 3)

By now I think it's safe to admit that I never really got into the Spice Girls thing. (This is Randy writing this, but I think Jim and Mitch will back me up.) The whole act was too contrived for me, too cute. Each member had her own little identity—Baby Spice, Lazy Spice, Crazy Spice, whatever.

But at least that can help us understand an important idea in this Adventure—the "signature sin." Chances are, you struggle with some temptation that has become a regular part of your life. It has worked its way into your identity, just like a Spice Girl, except it's Proud Mary or Lying John or Lusting Anthony or Angry Alisa.

Even if it's something you've kept secret from everyone else, you still know it's your pet sin. You try to stop, but you can't seem to break free. In defeat, you say, "Maybe that's just the way I am." And hey, there's a love-hate thing going on here—you're not really sure you want it gone anyway.

In our efforts to be the "real deal" with God, we need to get serious about these signature sins. We need to throw them down before Jesus and let God give us a new identity. It won't be easy, but God will give us power. He can set us free.

What makes it different this time? You may have tried to kick the habit before—you may even have a habit of trying to kick it. Chances are that's all based on guilt. Try focusing on love—love for yourself, love for God, love for those you care about. Sincerity and a honesty can go a long way.

Getting It Done:

Starting the third week, this journal will lead you through a six-step process designed to help you defeat your signature sin.

1. Name it. What is your signature sin? (If you have several, pick one.)

2. Agree with God that it's wrong. Whatever the reasons it got there, get honest about your habit. Forget the excuses (or get some help dealing with them), and take some responsibility for changing the way you do business.

3. Tell God you're sorry and accept his forgiveness. Grace is a wonderful thing. You don't have to wallow in guilt. Ask for forgiveness and accept God's grace.

4. Map out a strategy. If all you do is try to "beat" it, you are still letting it run your life. Replace your sin with something else. If your sin is an action or thought you do alone, get with some people. If you do it with certain people, stop hanging out with them. You know better than anyone what trips that temptation feeling in your head. Figure out a strategy to safely get past different points of the temptation, and stick to it.

5. Get help. Share your signature sin with a wise friend who can keep a secret or with a youth leader, pastor, parent, or other relative you trust. Such people can help you with advice, prayer, encouragement—and a swift kick when you need it. Sometimes the biggest weapon (and probably the hardest to do) is letting it out in the open.

6. Start over. What happens if you fail? Hey, this is hard stuff we're talking about. Take a deep breath, figure out what you could have done differently at different points of the temptation, adjust your strategy accordingly, and start over.

Care for Those Who Care for You

Every Day

What's your favorite TV show? (Or do you even have time to watch TV anymore?) Whatever it is, the next time you see it, stay tuned at the end to watch the credits roll. You'll see dozens of names of people you didn't even know were there. Yet they were absolutely essential to the show. Buffy wouldn't kill any vampires, Bart couldn't sass his folks, and Conan couldn't tease Andy if these people weren't doing their jobs behind the scenes.

Your life is like a TV show. And I'm not talking about comedic situations you get yourself into. I'm talking about all the people behind the scenes, people who care for you day after day.

Look around you; start rolling these credits in your mind: Parents, obviously. Perhaps your brothers or sisters or older relatives. Teachers, coaches, tutors, directors. I'm not saying you have to *like* everything these people do, but they are putting some effort into making you a better person, right? What about youth leaders, Sunday school teachers, pastors?

When you stop to notice, you see there's a whole industry, a Caring for You Enterprise, going on. Now, what have you done lately to care for those people? Maybe a lot, but probably not. It's easy to take those people for granted.

See if you can change that during this Adventure.

Getting It Done:

Every day of the Adventure, do something to care for someone who cares for you. Start by listing the people around you who are caring for you in some way. Ask God to help you compile that list. Consider family, friends, church workers, and so on. Just for kicks, add one person who doesn't care for you at all. (You probably won't come up with 50—that just means some of them will receive multiple kindnesses.)

Then do your stuff. One simple act of servant love each day. It doesn't have to be a big production number. Do a chore, drop a note, send a nice e-mail. Phone your grandparents, take your kid brother to the mall, say an honest thank you to a teacher.

Be creative. Be wacky. But be real. Show your appreciation in a bunch of different ways. Write a bunch of Bible verses on a T-shirt and give it to your youth leader. Secretly wash your pastor's car. Get a bunch of pals to go Christmas caroling at your best friend's house—even if Christmas is months away. You get the idea.

Get a piece of paper and start a list of 1 through 50. Each day, keep track of what you did. Then, fold up your list and keep it in your pocket, your wallet, your purse, or this journal. Just make sure you keep track of what you do every day. If you miss a day, try doing two the next day. If you get too far behind, just try to keep up. After the 50 days are up, fold the paper in half and staple it to this page.

Start Climbing the Walls

Once

WWJD.

These initials are adorning T-shirts, book bags, and bracelets all over the world. There are even kids with WWJD tattoos. What's it all about?

What Would Jesus Do?

A simple question that's hard to answer. It's often very tough to follow. But if you're serious about living what you say you believe, it's a question you've got to ask.

Jesus lived in a world different from ours. When he walked the earth, there were no CDs, PCs, or VCRs, no movies or microwave popcorn, no cash machines or car radios. But there's one thing his world had plenty of . . . prejudice. There were walls between races, between sexes, between religions. People were taught to stay away from those who were not like them.

Aren't you glad our world isn't like that?

In case you missed it, that was sarcasm. Our world *is* like that. We have huge walls separating people groups. Maybe you're lucky enough to pal around with people of different cultures; but even if you do, there's a wall somewhere you don't get over very often.

Here's the thing about Jesus, though. He always acted as if there were no walls. He climbed over them. He meets a Samaritan woman at a well—no problem. An Italian drill sergeant asks for a miracle—you got it. Jesus touched people with leprosy, partied with swindlers, and even showed kindness to prostitutes. He really was the real deal.

What would Jesus do about the walls of prejudice that divide our society? This answer's a slam dunk. Start climbing.

Getting It Done:

You just need to do one thing for this action step, but it's a big thing. Find a dividing wall in your world and climb it.

Start by looking around you at the social divisions in your school, community, or church. Are you shut off, for instance, from people of other races or cultures? Then choose this as the wall you'll climb.

Or perhaps you find stronger walls that keep you from taking the other sex seriously, that encourage you to hate people of other religions, that make it easy to ignore people with disabilities or elderly people. Choose the biggest wall you can find.

Now, how are you going to climb that wall? As Jesus did, through *relationship*. Try to start a relationship with one or more people on the other side of that wall.

This may not be easy. You may encounter resistance from the other side of the wall, and you won't get much encouragement from your side. Here's one idea: *Start by listening*. Ask questions. Learn what it's like to be on that side of the wall. Don't try to do any good deeds; just pay attention. Open your heart to the stories you've been neglecting.

It may not work, but do your best. Each step of the way, consider WWJD. What would Jesus do? And he promises to go with you.

The Real Deal:
Living What We Say We Believe

FRIDAY,

Read 2 Peter 1:3-9.

Date_____

1. What does Peter say God has promised us?

2. Rate the following qualities in yourself on a scale from 1-5:

Moral excellence _____

Knowing God _____

Self-control _____

Patient endurance _____

Godliness _____

Love for other Christians _____

Genuine love for everyone _____

3. If you were to tattoo one of these qualities somewhere on your body, which would it be, and where would you put it?

4. Which quality would you most like to improve on?

5. Briefly skim the reality checks and action steps (see p. 5) you will be going through on this Adventure. Do you think any of those will help you improve on what you answered for question 4? If so, which ones?

Unanswered ?s:

The Real Deal:
Living What We Say We Believe

SATURDAY,

Read John 15:1–17.

Date_____

1. Using the vine and branches imagery Jesus uses in this passage, which are you? Which is Jesus? What is God?

2. Why then do you think it is important to get deep with God?

3. List all the promises you can find in this passage. (Hint: We found 6; you may find fewer or possibly even more.)

4. Congratulations! You've won the Publisher's Craving House Sweepstakes. There's no money involved, but you can make a wish and get it. What would your wish be? What would your wish be for this Adventure?

Unanswered ?s:

Get Deep with God

T wo guys went to church to pray. One stood up and spoke out in that booming, important voice that some people pray with: "O Lord, I thank thee for making me as good and holy as I am."

The other guy just bowed down and prayed, "God, have mercy on me, a sinner."

When Jesus told this story, he shocked his listeners by declaring that it was the "sinner" and not the "holy" person who walked out of that room with a solid relationship with God (Luke 18:9-14).

In order to get real with God, you've got to stop bragging to him. The overwhelming message of the New Testament is that God only does business with sinners. If you think you can get to God's level by being good . . . well, you're wrong. And you'll waste a lot of effort.

Own up to your sinfulness. Then rely on God's power to transform you. Getting deep with God isn't something that requires a lot of work on our part, but we do have to make ourselves available to him. He'll do the digging, but you've got to be there to hold the shovel. Every day.

When Jesus talked about being the "bread of life" and the "living water," he wasn't just being cute. These are things we need to live on! We need to connect with Jesus regularly—day in, day out. He should be as much a part of our lives as the air we breathe.

The apostle Paul wrote, "I pray that from his glorious, unlimited resources he will give you mighty inner strength through his Holy Spirit. And I pray that Christ will be more and more at home in your hearts as you trust in him. May your roots go down deep into the soil of God's marvelous love. And may you have the power to understand, as all God's people should, how wide, how long, how high, and how deep his love really is. May you experience the love of Christ, though it is so great you will never fully understand it. Then you will be filled with the fullness of life and power that comes from God" (Ephesians 3:16-19).

That's what this reality check is all about. Filling ourselves up with God—every day, and even every moment.

Alyson took a good look at her life and decided she didn't like it. It wasn't anything in particular, just a slow, creeping dissatisfaction. She was a decent student at an average school with an okay family and a handful of friends she liked, more or less. Except her best friend, Jen. She really liked Jen, and Jen's life was as ordinary as her own. Alyson thought her life was like a—what was it?—a hologram. You could put your hand in the middle of it and not disturb a thing. It had no substance.

Alyson was a Christian—at age seven in Vacation Bible School she'd raised her hand to accept Jesus—and she still faithfully did all the church things she was expected to. But whenever she read about Elijah or Esther or that woman who poured perfume on Jesus, Alyson felt a door close inside her. Those people risked everything for the Lord. *It must be nice to have something worth taking a risk for.*

It was Tuesday night, and she had just calculated her fifteenth geometric proof—another useless assignment. She slammed her book shut. "Aaargh! It has to get better than this!" she screamed, launching the cat across the room and onto the dresser. The cat gave Alyson a look that said *I'll slap you later.* Above the cat a poster said, "If you feel far from God, guess who moved." Alyson thought that was really clever a couple of years ago. Now it just stung. "Well, don't look at *me!*" she snarled at the poster. "Nothing's moved in my life for years."

The cat leapt off the dresser, knocking Alyson's Bible to the floor. The cat sat on the Bible, curling her tail around her front paws. "All right, already! You think I can't take a hint?" Alyson pried the Bible from under the cat, who made a self-important exit from the room.

A church bulletin marked the spot of last Sunday's Bible study, Isaiah 40:31: "But those who wait on the Lord will find new strength. They will fly high on wings like eagles."

"Right," Alyson sighed. "Waiting is all I ever do. When will something *happen?* She stared at the words, hoping they would scramble and reassemble into something she could use. WAITONTHELORD.

Then she spoke out loud, startling herself with the pleading tone in her voice. "God, I don't get it. But if you want me to wait, I'll wait right here until you talk to me. I want to fly like an eagle, Lord, so . . . somehow . . . get my life moving, wouldja?"

She woke up the next morning on her bed, still clothed, curled around her Bible, the cat camped out on her head.

Check the box if you have completed the assignment.

❑ I read introductory pages 3–10.
❑ I did the warm-up days on pages 11–12.
❑ I read page 13 (Get Deep with God).

Coming Attractions

Reality Check 1: Get Deep with God

Daily Assignments:

- **Read the assigned Scripture passages** and answer the questions in the journal.
- **Breathe deep the breath of God** by taking a few deep breaths and praying the Real Deal Prayer: "What do you want to do today, Jesus?" (Action Step 1, p. 6).
- **Care for those who care for you** through acts of kindness (Action Step 4, p. 9).

Assignments for This Week:

- **Team up** with another Christian or three and get real with each other (Action Step 2, p. 7).
- **Bonus:** Memorize Bible passages that help you live what you say you believe.

Before the End:

- **Throw down your signature sin** by following the six steps that will help you defeat it (Action Step 3, p. 8).
- **Start climbing the walls** by starting a relationship with someone who has a different story from yours (Action Step 5, p. 10).

Pocket the Pack

The Real Deal Scripture Pack

This handy pack gives you a great way to carry God's breath with you—in your pocket or in your head. You can carry 22 Adventure Bible verses and The Real Deal Prayer with you wherever you go. And the pack is a great tool to help you memorize some of God's Word—then you really will be able to breathe deep the breath of God.

Ask for this resource at your church, or call Mainstay Church Resources at 1-800-224-2735. (See the order form on page 80.)

Get Deep with God

Day 1
SUNDAY,

Read Luke 10:38–42.

Date_____

1. What was Mary's priority in this passage? How about Martha's?

2. What are some things in your life that distract you from spending time with God?

❑ Can't miss *ER*.
❑ Hangin' with my friends.
❑ History homework is just so thrilling.
❑ Sports.

❑ Chores.
❑ Cleaning my room.
❑ My hobbies.
❑ Other_____ .

❑ Waxing my snowboard, man.

3. Action Step 1 in this Adventure (breathe deep the breath of God, see p. 6) is all about paying attention to God. What can you do to make sure distractions don't keep you from paying attention to God every day?

4. If you haven't started Action Step 1 yet, take some time now to do so, and then come back to this question. If you have, what was it like?

Unanswered ?s:

Get Deep with God

Day 2
MONDAY,

Read Psalm 63.

Date_____

1. Have you ever felt the "thirst" or "longing" for God that David is talking about in this psalm? Explain.

2. Your best friend reads this psalm to you and says that it was a poem he or she wrote about God. Then he or she asks you how well his or her love and desire to be intimate with God came through. Put a mark on the following scale to answer the question (1 being none, and 10 being as much as possible).

```
1     2     3     4     5     6     7     8     9     10
+-----+-----+-----+-----+-----+-----+-----+-----+-----+
```

3. If you were to put your desire to spend intimate time with God on the same scale, where would you put yourself?

```
1     2     3     4     5     6     7     8     9     10
+-----+-----+-----+-----+-----+-----+-----+-----+-----+
```

4. Now rate what percentage of time you are actually intimate with God.

```
1     2     3     4     5     6     7     8     9     10
+-----+-----+-----+-----+-----+-----+-----+-----+-----+
```

5. Take some time to look over 3 three scales above. Where would you realistically like the scale for question 4 to be by the end of this Adventure?

```
1     2     3     4     5     6     7     8     9     10
+-----+-----+-----+-----+-----+-----+-----+-----+-----+
```

Unanswered ?s:

Get Deep with God

Day 3
TUESDAY,

Read Revelation 2:1–7.

Date_____

1. What is it the church at Ephesus is warned about in this passage?

2. Put a point on the graph that shows the height of your enthusiasm when Jesus first became real to you. Then, put another point that shows where you are now.

LOVE

FIRST/NOW

3. Did you do things differently at the time of your "first love" with Jesus? Explain.

4. Was it important for you to spend intimate time "breathing the breath of God" at that point in your life? Is there any difference now? Explain.

5. What is the promise listed at the end of this passage?

Unanswered ?s:

Get Deep with God

Day 4
WEDNESDAY,

Read 1 John 1:1–10.

Date_____

1. What is the relationship in your life between fellowship with God and walking in "the darkness" (NIV)?

2. Do you find you spend more or less time than usual with God when you try to hide or ignore your guilt?

3. According to verse 9, what is needed to get back on track with God?

4. Why, then, do you think it is important to be "real" with God?

5. Is there something in your life that is keeping you at a distance from God? If you answered yes, what step can you take to address that?

Unanswered ?s:

Get Deep with God

Day 5
THURSDAY,

Read Mark 1:32–39.

Date_____

1. If Simon and his companions had had their way, what do you think Jesus would have been doing instead of praying?

2. After reading this passage, how important do you think it was for Jesus to spend time with his Father? Why do you think it was important?

3. Fill in this pie chart with how you spend your time. Make sure to include a "slice" for how much time you spend with Jesus.

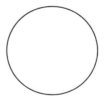

4. Are there distractions that are keeping you from "breathing deep the breath of God"? If so, what is your plan for keeping time with Jesus a priority?

5. How big would you like that time with Jesus "slice of pie" to be?

Unanswered ?s:

Get Deep with God

Day 6
FRIDAY,

Read Psalm 73:25–28.

Date_____

1. In your own words, why is it good to be near God?

2. Briefly describe the time you have spent with God over the last week.

3. Are you ready to promise to pay attention to God every day? If yes, realistically how would you like to keep your focus? How much time would you like to promise to spend on this journal? How about beyond this Adventure (e.g., I promise to spend 10 minutes alone with God each day for the next 50, 60, or 90 days)? If no, would you like to think about it more and decide later (you'll have more opportunities to come back to this during the Adventure)?

4. If you're ready to make a promise, fill in the blanks (or write your own promise) and sign and date it. If you decide to make a promise down the road, come back and do this later.

Note: Promises are meant to be kept, but they are also a process. Don't get down if you don't live up to your end of the bargain. Instead, grab on to God's grace and keep going. These promises are the real deal, and many of them can be a lifelong process of learning to live with Jesus.

I promise to spend _____ *alone with God each day for* _____ *days.*

Signed: _____   Date: _____

Unanswered ?s:

Get Real with Each Other

I t was an exciting time. The church was just starting out, and everybody was giving sacrificially to get it going. One couple, we'll call them Andy and Sally, sold their home and brought the money to the church leaders. Everyone was very impressed with their sizable gift—but there was one problem.

They were only giving half of their selling price to the church—yet they claimed it was the whole amount. They were lying to the church, trying to seem more spiritual than they were.

So God struck them dead.

Seriously! Read it for yourself in Acts 5. The punishment seems pretty harsh, but it was important for God to deal swiftly with dishonesty. The story makes it clear that "Andy and Sally" didn't have to give any more than they gave, but they should have been honest about it. The church would be built on truth, not lies.

What if God did the same thing today whenever Christians pretend to be more spiritual than they really are? People would be struck dead all over the place. Our churches would look like episodes of *The X Files*.

Why can't we be real with each other? Why do we insist on playing those "I'm okay, you're okay" games? Why can't we admit our failures and share our struggles? Our faith is built on God's forgiveness; we rely on his grace. It's never about our own holiness. So why should we act as if we have it all together when we don't?

The Bible says, "Confess your sins to each other and pray for each other so that you may be healed" (James 5:16). As you humbly acknowledge your own struggles, you'll create an atmosphere where others will be able to open up to you. Then you can pray with each other and for each other. "So don't condemn each other anymore," the apostle Paul wrote. "Decide instead to live in such a way that you will not put an obstacle in another Christian's path" (Romans 14:13).

The stumbling block may be the act you're putting on, pretending you're a perfect Christian when you're not. Try being honest about who you are, about where you are in your relationship with Christ. Then you'll be able to get help from others, and you can help those who are honest with you.

Saturdays, like clockwork, Alyson met Jen for bagels at the mall. Alyson was quiet. Jen looked at her. "So . . . ?" Jen said. "You haven't called me since Monday. What's up?" (This was one of life's great imbalances. Jen never called; but if Alyson didn't call every couple of days, Jen got all pouty.)

"So what's up?" Jen repeated. "You find a man, or what?"

"I wish."

"Then . . . you're just ignoring me."

"I've been busy, okay?"

Jen looked hurt. The truth was, Alyson was busy repeating the Bible-staring routine she had started on Tuesday night. Wednesday, God didn't exactly say anything to her, but Alyson was determined. She thumbed through her Bible, looking at different verses, trying to see them in new ways. She fell asleep with her Bible open. Thursday, Alyson woke with a strange, pleasant feeling of wholeness. Then, third period, one of those verses flashed into her mind. (Worrying about a history quiz, she recalled Isaiah 41:10: "Don't be afraid, I am with you.") Thursday night, she looked at some new verses, trying to see them from God's perspective. This opened all sorts of new meaning. By Friday night Alyson was almost . . . well, excited! She fell asleep with her Bible open again.

Saturday, Alyson slept late and woke up grumpy.

"You're busy, then." Jen said, prying. "Me, too. Lotta homework?"

Alyson felt cornered. She couldn't bring herself to tell Jen what was going on. Sure, Jen was a Christian, too, but was this normal? Would Jen understand? Alyson thought not.

"Yeah," Alyson hemmed. "Homework."

Well, it wasn't exactly a *lie*. She did have homework those nights—and she was at home and her meditation was sort of "work."

"That never stopped you before," Jen said in her *why-do-you-hate-me?* voice. Why couldn't she just drop it?

But, then, why couldn't Alyson talk honestly with her best friend about this really cool thing going on in her life? If it was a new boyfriend, they'd be gabbing about it day and night. Why should a relationship with God be any different?

"Well, to be honest," Alyson began, "it's not just homework. . . ."

Check the box if you have completed the assignment.

❏ I did Days 1–6.

❏ I breathed deep the breath of God.

❏ I cared for those who care for me.

❏ I teamed up with another Christian.

❏ I read page 22 (Get Real with Each Other).

Coming Attractions

Reality Check 2: Get Real with Each Other

Daily Assignments:

• **Read the assigned Scripture passages** and answer the questions in the journal.

• **Breathe deep the Breath of God** by taking a few deep breaths and pray ing the Real Deal Prayer: "What do you want to do today, Jesus?" (Action Step 1, p. 6).

• **Care for those who care for you** through acts of kindness (Action Step 4, p. 9).

Assignments for This Week:

• **Team up** with another Christian or three and get real with each other (Action Step 2, p. 7).

• **Bonus:** Memorize Bible passages that help you live what you say you believe.

Before the End:

• **Throw down your signature sin** by following the six steps that will help you defeat it (Action Step 3, p. 8).

• **Start climbing the walls** by starting a relationship with someone who has a different story from yours (Action Step 5, p. 10).

Get Real with Each Other

Days 7&8

SATURDAY/SUNDAY,

Read Proverbs 27:6, 9, 17.

Date_____

1. You're designing a poster for your room based on these verses. What kind of picture do you use, and what does the poster say?

2. Has there been a time in your life when you've appreciated the honesty of a friend confronting you, even when it hurt to hear it?

3. Has there been a time in your life when you've honestly confronted a friend, even when you knew it would be hard for him or her to hear?

4. Do you have friends who "sharpen" you? Explain. Are you a friend who "sharpens" others?

5. What things can you do to make sure that when you "team up" (Action Step 2) for this Adventure, you get "real" enough to sharpen each other?

Unanswered ?s:

Get Real with Each Other

Day 9
MONDAY,

Read Romans 1:11–12.

Date_____

1. Write eight lines of a script for *Promised Land*, or *Touched by an Angel*, (pick one), in which the characters are "mutually encouraging."

2. What relationships do you have that are "mutually encouraging"?

3. What does "getting real" with your friends have to do with "mutual encouragement"?

4. Have you found it hard or easy to "get real" with your friends? Has it been a good thing or a bad thing? Explain.

Unanswered ?s:

Get Real with Each Other

Day 10
TUESDAY,

Read Daniel 1:1–21.

Date_____

1. How did God help the young men in this passage (verse 17)?

2. These four friends teamed up together to keep a promise to God about their diet. In what ways do you think these four friends helped each other?

3. What qualities do you look for in a friend?

4. How important is his or her ability to help you keep your promises or follow God?

5. Have you decided already who you want to "team up" with for Action Step 2 (p. 7)? What if they can't partner with you? Have you met already? How did it go?

Unanswered ?s:

Get Real with Each Other

Day 11

WEDNESDAY,

Read James 5:13–20.

Date_____

1. What does this passage say about friendship?

2. "Confessing sins" and "praying for each other" can be a pretty tough thing to do with your friends. Can you think of any times in the past when you have done either of these things? Explain.

3. What do you think would happen if you were "real" enough with your friends to constantly confess your sins together and pray for each other? Is this something you would like to try?

4. Is there anything you shouldn't confess to others?

5. How would it change the relationships on *Party of Five* or *Friends* if they confessed their faults to one another?

Unanswered ?s:

Get Real with Each Other

Day 12
Thursday,

Read 1 Samuel 20:1–17.

Date_____

1. List the promises made by David and Jonathan to each other in this passage.

2. Read the rest of this story (verses 18–42). What happened as a result of David and Jonathan's promises? How would it have been different if they were not as "real" and honest with each other as they were?

3. What can you do to make sure the friends you've teamed up with trust you and believe your promises?

4. Is there anything you haven't shared with your "team" that you feel may be important? What would it take to be able to share this? How can you get to that point of "getting real"?

5. David and Jonathan were a great pair of friends. What's your favorite duo from TV, the movies, music, or history? How is their partnership like or unlike that of David and Jonathan?

Unanswered ?s:

Get Real with Each Other

Day 13
FRIDAY,

Read Ecclesiastes 4:9–12.   **Date**_____

1. Based on these verses, write a 30-second commercial for friendship, using the phrase *I've fallen, and I can't get up.*

2. Is there something you need a friend's help with that you haven't asked for yet? Who would be a person you could go to who would "help you up"?

3. Considering the Bible passages you've read this past week (feel free to review them if you would like to), how important is it to you to "get real" with your friends and to "team up"?

4. Are you ready to promise to "team up" and "get real" with your friends? If yes, make your promise in question 5. If no, would you like to think about it more and decide later (you'll have more opportunities to come back to this during the Adventure)?

5. Sign your name and fill in the date below if you're ready to make this promise (or write your own promise). If you decide to make a promise down the road, come back and do this later.

I promise to be honest and make friendships really count.

Signed: _____ Date: _____

Unanswered ?s:

Get Some Help with the Hard Stuff

J ustin was stumped by his math homework, stumped as in clueless about the final problem. But Justin was nothing if not focused. His buddy Dave called. Justin let the machine get it. Justin kept working the equation. Dave called again. The message sounded urgent. It would have to wait.

After three and half hours, Justin saw the solution. "Aha! I need to find the cotangent first." He was right; the rest of the numbers fell into place. Triumphantly, he called Dave. "Sorry, man, I was stuck on that last problem."

"Well, yeah," Dave replied. "That's why I called. On the way out of class, Mr. C told us the key to the last problem was the cotangent. You left class so fast, I wasn't sure you heard him. He said it would be almost impossible without knowing that."

"Unbelievable! Three and a half hours of needless agony. If I'd just picked up the stupid phone! I'm such an imbecile! It was right there! I'm so stupid. . . ."

The same thing happens with our spiritual struggles. You may be wrestling with alcohol, drugs, or sex. You may be fighting attitudes like pride, rebellion, hatred, or low self-esteem. You may slam up against the same sins day after day, week after week. How can you solve this problem?

It's the cotangent.

No, seriously, I (Randy) don't know what the key will be for you, but I know it rests with God, and not with your own efforts. He's leaving messages for you—will you ever pick up the phone? Will you take advantage of his help?

The apostle Paul had struggles of his own, and he writes an amazing description. "I don't understand myself at all, for I really want to do what is right, but I don't do it. Instead, I do the very thing I hate. . . . No matter which way I turn, I can't make myself do right. I want to, but I can't. When I want to do good, I don't. And when I try not to do wrong, I do it anyway. . . . Oh, what a miserable person I am! Who will free me from this life that is dominated by sin? Thank God! The answer is in Jesus Christ our Lord" (Romans 7:15–25).

Life is harder than any math homework. Even a great Christian like Paul found that out. The answer lies not in our own lonely efforts but in the power of Christ.

He has power to forgive the mistakes we make, the power to transform our priorities, the power to speak to us in any situation, the power to forgive us again when we screw up again, and the power to help us make good choices. Thank God!

Jen couldn't stop thinking about what Alyson told her. Every night, finishing her homework and then reading her Bible, waiting. It seemed funny at first, and Jen joked about it. But Alyson was serious. It made Jen think about her own relationship with God. Stagnant, at best.

The folks at church talked a lot about God's power, but Jen didn't feel it. Her life could sure use a shot of power about now.

Friday night, as usual, Jen found herself alone with Brian, at his place. His folks were always out late on Fridays. Jen felt guilty about what they did together, but she couldn't seem to stop. She loved Brian and was afraid she'd lose him. They went further and further, and she felt worse and worse. Every Saturday she hated herself and swore to break it off before it was too late—even if it cost her the relationship. Then Brian would call, and she'd be caught up again in her desire for him.

As things progressed with Brian, Jen found it harder to pray. She felt God must be terribly disappointed. Her prayers seemed to splat against the ceiling. How could God do anything when she kept disobeying him?

After hearing Alyson's story, Jen tried to read the Bible, praying for God's power. But the next Friday night, she lost the battle again, in a humiliating defeat. Her Saturday morning remorse was worse than ever. She started crying the moment her eyes opened. She had tried praying, and it didn't work. Had God given up on her?

Eating bagels with Alyson, Jen finally confessed her struggle. She had avoided the subject for a long time, afraid Alyson wouldn't want anything to do with her. Now she felt she had nothing to lose. "Ally . . . I, uh, have this problem, sort of," she stammered, "with Brian."

Alyson looked sad as she heard Jen's story. Finally, Alyson said, "I'm really sorry for your pain, Jen. I haven't been in your shoes, exactly, but, as you know, I have trouble telling the truth sometimes—all the time." Jen nodded sadly, and Alyson brightened. "Lookit, I'll pray for you," she said. "Every night, when I'm spending time with God, I'll talk to him about you. Okay? I know that sounds kind of—"

Jen raised her hand to stop Alyson. "No, it's great," she said quietly. "I don't think my prayers work."

A thought popped into Alyson's head. "Why don't we do something this Friday? Go to a movie or something."

"But Brian—"

"Exactly. If he wants to come too, great. But let's give you someplace to be—besides his house."

Check the box if you have completed the assignment.

❑ I did Days 7–13.
❑ I breathed deep the breath of God.
❑ I cared for those who care for me.
❑ I teamed up with another Christian.
❑ I read page 31 (Get Some Help with the Hard Stuff).

Coming Attractions

Reality Check 3: Get Some Help with the Hard Stuff

Daily Assignments:

- **Read the assigned Bible passages** and answer the questions in the journal.
- **Breathe deep the breath of God** by taking a few deep breaths and praying the Real Deal Prayer: "What do you want to do today, Jesus?" (Action Step 1, p. 6).
- **Care for those who care for you** through acts of kindness. (Action Step 4, p. 9).

Assignments for This Week:

- **Team up** with another Christian or three and get real with each other (Action Step 2, p. 7).
- **Throw down your signature sin** by following the six steps that will help you defeat it (Action Step 3, p. 8).
- **Bonus:** Memorize Bible passages that help you live what you say you believe.

Before the End:

- **Start climbing the walls** by starting a relationship with someone who has a different story from yours (Action Step 5, p. 10).

Get Some Help with the Hard Stuff

Days 14&15
SATURDAY/SUNDAY,

Date_____

Read Hebrews 12:1—3.

1. What four things does this passage give us to do?

2. Take a moment to think about and pray for the perseverance it will take for you to throw down your signature sin.

3. Now, go back and read through Action Step 3, throw down your signature sin, on page 8. What do you need to do to assure that you are ready and serious about this action step?

4. You can start Action Step 3 by naming the signature sin you would like to throw down during this Adventure. Write it below.

Unanswered ?s:

Get Some Help
with the Hard Stuff

Day 16
MONDAY,

Read Genesis 39:1–23.   **Date**_____

1. What were the reasons Joseph gave for resisting temptation?
❑ Trying to stay focused on his new business.
❑ Bad hair day.
❑ A get-rich-quick scam.
❑ She just wasn't his type.
❑ Other _____.

2. What are your reasons for throwing down your signature sin?

3. The second step for Action Step 3 is agreeing with God that your signature sin is wrong. Take a moment to think about this, and then write a short prayer to God below.

4. Throwing down your signature sin will not be easy, and no one expects you to be perfect. Have you faced any struggles so far this week? If so, what? (Remember to go back often and read the six steps for Action Step 3 on page 8.)

Unanswered ?s:

Get Some Help
with the Hard Stuff

Day 17
TUESDAY,

Read Romans 6:12–23.   **Date**_____

1. According to this passage, why does sin no longer control the way believers live?

2. Verse 18 says, "Now you are free from sin . . . and you have become slaves to your new master, righteousness." What do you think that means? How do you feel about that?

3. Christ died on the cross so that your sins could be forgiven. God's grace is available to you! You do not have to carry your guilt around. If this doesn't make sense to you, or if this is new to you, find someone to talk about it with. (Your youth leader, pastor, or a trusted Christian friend may be good choices for this.)

4. Step 3 in Action Step 3 is to tell God you're sorry about your sin and to accept his forgiveness. If you are ready to do that, take a moment and write a short prayer to God.

5. Do something symbolic to get rid of your guilt. Here are some ideas:

• Write your sin on paper and burn it.
• Pour a little dirt in your bathtub and scour it clean.
• Type everything you feel guilty about in a computer file and delete it.

Unanswered ?s:

Get Some Help
with the Hard Stuff

Day 18
WEDNESDAY,

Read Psalm 119:9–16.

Date_____

1. In your own words, how can a young man or woman stay pure?

2. The writer of this psalm says that he has hidden the Word of God in his heart as protection against sinning. Are there any Bible verses you know of that could help you in your struggle to throw down your signature sin? If so, write them down here. If not, take some time to review the verses you've read so far for this Adventure and see if any of them work for you. (It may help you to carry around The Real Deal Scripture Pack or to try to memorize some of the Bible passages for this Adventure.)

3. Step 4 for Action Step 3 is to map out a strategy for throwing down your signature sin. If you haven't already done this, take some time to think about it. When you're ready, write your strategy here. (For help with developing a strategy, go back and read Action Step 3 on p. 8.)

4. If you need some more time to think or pray about throwing down your signature sin, take some time to do so now. It may also be helpful to go back and read page 8 and also pages 31–32.

Unanswered ?s:

Get Some Help
with the Hard Stuff

Day 19
THURSDAY,

Read Colossians 3:1–17.

Date_____

1. What are three "sinful, earthly things lurking within you"?

2. What does it mean to "put to death the sinful, earthly things lurking within you"?

3. Make a list from this passage of what we are to do instead.

4. Possibly the hardest part of Action Step 3 is Step 5: Get some help. But it can also make the biggest difference. Who have you talked to, or who would you like to talk to, about your signature sin? If you haven't talked to someone yet about your signature sin, what can you do to make that happen?

5. Speaking of getting some help . . . by this time you should be well on your way with Action Step 2: team up. How has it helped you to "get real" with your team? What has been hard for you?

Unanswered ?s:

Get Some Help
with the Hard Stuff

Day 20

FRIDAY,

Date_____

Read Philippians 4:6–9.

1. What do you identify with the following words from verse 8?

True _____ Lovely_____
Honorable_____ Admirable _____
Right_____ Excellent _____
Pure _____ Worthy_____

2. Verse 7 says, "If you do this, you will experience God's peace." Have you felt any peace as you've tried to throw down your "signature sin"? Explain.

3. Signature sins are not easy to throw down. Maybe you are having a hard time with it, or maybe you've given up. Step 6 for Action Step 3 is to start over. You may need to go back and read page 8 again and get a fresh start. You may also want to reevaluate the strategy you developed for Step 4. Or maybe, if you haven't already, it's time to try Step 5 and get some help with this. What do you think you need to do?

4. Are you ready to promise to "get some help with the hard stuff" and to "throw down your signature sin"? If yes, make your promise in question 5. If no, would you like to think about it more and decide later (you'll have more opportunities to come back to this during the Adventure)?

5. Sign your name and fill in the date below if you're ready to make this promise (or write your own promise). If you decide to make a promise down the road, come back and do this later.

I promise to practice living a life that pleases God.

Signed: _____ Date: _____

Unanswered ?s:

Get Right with Your Family

E ven Jesus had problems with his family. They took a trip to Jerusalem when he was a kid, and somehow left him at the Temple when they went home. Of course, they blamed him. "We were worried sick about you." You know the routine.

"Hey, look," Jesus answered. "I'm what?—12 years old now? Don't you know I gotta be hangin' with the holy men?" (We're paraphrasing a little, but read it for yourself in Luke 2:41–52.)

Even when Jesus reached adulthood, his mother was still telling him what to do (John 2:3). His own family was very slow to believe in him; they even tried to curtail his ministry (Mark 3:21; John 7:3–5). This certainly isn't a knock against Jesus, and it's not intended as a criticism of his family. The point is: Nobody grows up in a perfect family. Put any group of people together that close for that many years, and there are going to be some quarrels, some misunderstandings, some fights—even if you are the Messiah.

But your family can also be your best resource, your strongest ally, your closest confidant.

It's easy, in your teenage years, to take your family for granted. Even Christians can develop a love-hate relationship that looks more like hate than love. An important part of the growing-up process is to break free from your family, to make your own choices. Of course, it's hard for your folks to let you do that.

The Bible has a number of ideas about child-parent relations. The most obvious is, "Children, obey your parents" (Ephesians 6:1). That's simple enough. But even this is set in a context of give-and-take. The whole section begins with a challenge to *everybody* to "submit to one another out of reverence for Christ" (Ephesians 5:21), and parents are urged not to "exasperate" their kids. In the same passage, slaves are urged to serve their masters *as if they were serving Christ*. If you feel like a slave in your own home, that's a verse for you.

The Book of Proverbs regularly tells you to follow your parents' instruction because they're probably wiser than you are. It may not seem that way now, but they'll probably seem wiser as you get older.

Yet the best biblical word about families is in the Ten Commandments: "*Honor* your father and mother." This is more than mere obedience. It means treating them with respect, accepting them as human beings, caring about how they feel.

As you seek to be a Real Deal Christian, you need to shore up the home front. We know many kids have less-than-perfect home situations these days, but do your best to honor those in your own home, treating them as you would treat Christ himself.

Helping Jen made Alyson feel great. It gave her life new meaning. Brian agreed to join them for a Friday night movie, but he was not happy about it. Then, Wednesday morning, Alyson's mom dropped a bombshell. "Ally, we need you to baby-sit the girls Friday."

"MOM!" Alyson exploded. Deep breath. "Mom, I can't. I'm going out with Jen."

Mom dug in her heels. "Your brother has a game, Alyson. I understand you want to go out with Jen, but I need you to understand that I need you here."

"But you *DON'T* understand!"

But she was gone, out the door and off to work. She didn't understand, but there would be no further discussion, and Alyson would change her plans accordingly. *If she had any clue . . . any inkling how important this is. . . .* But she didn't, and she never would. *What's the use?*

Alyson fumed all day. She ate dinner with the family in stony silence and went to her room quickly. Her Bible reading was lousy; she could only see red.

Jen took the news well. She decided she'd still see a movie with Brian, but she'd "really try" not to go back to his place. Throughout the day, Alyson felt hopeless, and Thursday was no better. She didn't even try reading her Bible.

Friday night, after Alyson put her sisters to bed, she picked up her Bible again. Still angry at her mom, worried about Jen, and feeling sorry for herself, she landed on the story of the Prodigal Son.

What made this guy run away from home? Parents who wouldn't listen? How did he feel when the money was gone, when he was feeding pigs? Angry at the world, no doubt. But then he came to his senses and went home to the comfort in his father's open arms. Alyson pictured God's great arms thrown wide to greet her. She wondered whether her parents would welcome her back if she ran away. Probably.

Her mind kept turning around this story. Why didn't the father send out search parties? Maybe he had to wait until the boy *decided* to come home.

The chirping phone brought her back to the present.

"Guess where I am." It was Jen. "I'm home!" she proclaimed, not giving Alyson a chance to answer.

"*Your* home, not Brian's?"

"He just dropped me off."

Alyson glanced at the clock. "It's only 9:42."

"Short movie, and then I came straight home." Alyson heard her friend draw a deep breath. "I was strong, Al. Even without you there! I said no."

"Great. Really."

"That was the right thing, wasn't it?"

Even over this cheap phone, Alyson heard Jen's strength slipping. "Absolutely," she assured her. "I'm really in a yucky mood. Could you come over?"

"Now? Be there in ten."

Check the box if you have completed the assignment.

❑ I did Days 14–20.

❑ I breathed deep the breath of God.

❑ I cared for those who care for me.

❑ I teamed up with another Christian.

❑ I'm working on throwing down my signature sin.

❑ I read page 40 (Get Right with Your Family).

Coming Attractions

Reality Check 4: Get Right with Your Family

Daily Assignments:
- **Read the assigned Bible passages** and answer the questions in the journal.
- **Breathe deep the breath of God** by taking a few deep breaths and praying the Real Deal Prayer: "What do you want to do today, Jesus?" (Action Step 1, p. 6).
- **Care for those who care for you** through acts of kindness (Action Step 4, p. 9).

Assignments for This Week:
- **Team up** with another Christian or three and get real with each other (Action Step 2, p. 7).
- **Throw down your signature sin** by following the six steps that will help you defeat it (Action Step 3, p. 8).
- **Bonus:** Memorize Bible passages that help you live what you say you believe.

Before the End:
- **Start climbing the walls** by starting a relationship with someone who has a different story from yours (Action Step 5, p. 10).

Get Right with Your Family

Days 21&22

SATURDAY/SUNDAY,

Read Matthew 20:20–28.

Date_____

1. What does this passage leave you thinking?
❑ I want to be first.
❑ I'm not sure I want that cup.
❑ Those disciples were always fighting.
❑ Servant and slave is a bit much, isn't it?
❑ I want to serve.
❑ Other _____ .

2. In what ways do you think you could be a servant to the different members of your family?

3. How are the different members of your family servants to you?

4. Action Step 4 (p. 9) is to do some act of kindness every day for those who care for you. This week, try to serve your family with this action step. What ideas do you have for what you could do?

Unanswered ?s:

Get Right with Your Family

Day 23

MONDAY,

Read Esther 2:5–11.

Date_____

1. In what ways did Mordecai care for his cousin Esther?

2. If this story were part of a TV show that is on today, what show do you think it would be? What would the story be?

3. Make a list of your family members, including your extended family, who care for you.

4. Now make a list of all the things members of your family do for you. Circle the three things you appreciate the most.

5. What could you do to show your appreciation to your family?

Unanswered ?s:

Get Right with Your Family

Day 24
TUESDAY,

Read Ephesians 5:21—6:4.

Date_____

1. What is the promise in this passage to children who obey their parents?

2. What is the responsibility given to parents in this passage?

3. Is there anything in this passage that you don't like? If yes, what is it, and what don't you like about it? Is there someone you could talk to about it?

4. Are there times when you shouldn't obey your parents? Explain.

5. Is there something specific you need to do or talk about in order to "get right with your family"? Explain.

Unanswered ?s:

Get Right with Your Family

Day 25
WEDNESDAY,

Read Genesis 50:15–21.

Date_____

1. Joseph forgave his brothers for the wrong they did him. Are there issues you need to consider forgiving a brother or sister for? How about your mother or father? If so, what are they?

2. What have you done this week to care for those who care for you?

3. What other ideas do you have to care for those who care for you?

4. How are you doing with the other action steps (breathe deep the breath of God, team up, and throw down your signature sin)? If you haven't been following too closely, why not start fresh today?

5. Right here on this page, write a note to some family member you need to get right with. If you had that person's undivided attention, what would you say?

Unanswered ?s:

Get Right with Your Family

DAY 26

Day 26
THURSDAY,

Read Deuteronomy 6:1–9.

Date_____

1. What responsibilities are given to parents in this passage?

2. Which of these responsibilities are most challenging? Rank them, hardest to easiest.

3. How could you help your family live up to those responsibilities? Or how do you feel you will live up to those responsibilities, if you are ever a parent?

4. Is your signature sin something you could possibly discuss with your family? If it is, how would you go about doing that and getting their help?

5. How have you been doing with the promises you've made during this Adventure? If there are promises you wanted to think about a little more, have you come to any decisions? If you are ready to make any of the promises you wanted to come back to, now would be a good time to do that.

Unanswered ?s:

Get Right with Your Family

Day 27
FRIDAY,
Date_____

Read 2 Samuel 9:1–13.

1. As we learned earlier in 1 Samuel 20:1–17 (Day 12), David thought of his friend Jonathan as a brother and made many promises to him. This passage shows David keeping his promises. What does this say about the importance David placed on promises?

2. How important to you are promises you make to people? Would you go out of your way to keep a promise?

3. How do you feel about promises that others make to you? Do you believe them? Do you trust that their promises are true?

4. Are you ready to promise to "get right with your family" and to "care for those who care for you"? If yes, make your promise in question 5. If no, would you like to think about it more and decide later? Are there any promises you skipped that you would like to go back to and reconsider?

5. Sign your name and fill in the date below if you're ready to make this promise (or write your own promise). If you decide to make a promise down the road, come back and do this later.

I promise to make family relationships a priority.

Signed: _____ Date: _____

Unanswered ?s:

Get Pumped About God's Work

Let's go back to that first church meeting on the day of Pentecost (Acts 2). The disciples are gathered in that upper room when—*whoosh!*—the Holy Spirit comes upon them, filling them with power. Soon they're all speaking to everyone around them in whatever language they need. Peter gathers a crowd and speaks mightily about the risen Jesus. Three thousand people become Christians that day.

And I (Randy) am guessing there's a bunch of teenagers in the back row of that upper room, saying, "Church is so dull. Why doesn't anything ever happen around here?"

A cheap shot, I know. And the truth is that some churches *are* dull, especially for teens. Often churches operate at a pace designed for sixty-year-olds, rather than sixteen-year-olds. So you're excused if you have to stifle a yawn now and then.

But, like it or not, God chooses to work through his church. That means you and me, but it also means First Methodist and Community Baptist and Faith Presbyterian. God is working through your pastor and youth leader and Sunday school teacher, even if they try to hide it. And God's work is always something to get excited about.

Here are a few quick ideas on how to keep your interest up in what God's doing, even if your church is less than thrilling.

Keep worshiping. Worship starts in the heart, *your* heart. Go to your worship service with a sincere desire to please God, and you'll begin to see that others have that same desire. If the service is too slow, let your mind wander—but let it wander through God's green pastures. Meditate on the hymns, the stained-glass windows, or how God will help you in the coming week.

Play detective. You may need to hunt for God's exciting activity in your church, but you'll find it. Ask people how their faith is growing. Look for all the behind-the-scenes ways people serve. Ask the head usher why he or she's been doing that for 50 years—you will learn some of the terrific stories behind your church.

Add yourself to the mix. The church is a collection of people with different gifts (1 Corinthians 12). You have as much right as anybody to affect what happens there. So make suggestions, participate in church meetings, plan new activities. Remember Paul's advice to Timothy: "Don't let anyone look down on you because you are young, but set an example" (1 Timothy 4:12, NIV).

Watch your attitude. Don't get cynical about church. Don't start passing judgment all the time. Keep a humble mindset (Philippians 2:3–11).

Honor your leaders. Show appreciation for your preachers and teachers and planners, even if you don't always agree with them. They're giving a lot of time and effort to serve God and build the church. Say thank you.

The rhythmic pounding finally registered with Mike. The man with claws had followed him all night. Now he was at the door. Mike burrowed deeper beneath the covers. *Wait a second. Covers . . . bed . . . sleep . . . it's a dream.* Back to sleep then. But the pounding continued. Alyson!

"Go away," Mike moaned.

"Rise and shine, dipswitch! We leave for church in half an hour."

Church, he thought. *Sunday . . . no school . . . good.*

The pounding continued. "Are you awake, or what?"

"Yarrrrhhhhhh!" Mike replied.

The door opened a crack, and Alyson poked her head in. "Half an hour, Mikey. Get moving."

"Not going," Mike muttered, pulling the covers over his head.

"Not acceptable."

"Too tired," he moaned.

"You're breakin' my heart, Mr. Watch-TV-Till-Two-AM."

Mike peeked from under the sheets. "Who died and made you Mom?"

"Mom and Dad already left for the choir thingy. They told me to get you going. You now have twenty- . . . eight minutes to shower, dress, and, let's see, I think you already shaved this month. . . ."

"I'm sick," Mike said blankly, covering his head.

This wasn't working. A few weeks ago, it wouldn't have mattered. She had faked illness herself. But she felt different now.

"Listen, Mike," she said in a softer tone. "You have an engraved invitation to worship the Creator of the universe. Unlovable as you can be sometimes, you're still invited to the party. I mean, who knows? Going to church today could change your life."

Mike pulled the covers off his head. "What's the deal with you?" he spat. "I'm not going, okay? I'll deal with Mom and Dad. Now get outa my room." He disappeared beneath the sheets again.

"I know it's boring sometimes. But if you really—"

Mike's head surfaced, cutting Alyson off in mid-sentence. "I already heard a sermon, Alyson. Loud and clear. Thanks for saving me the trip. C-ya."

With that, Mike turned his back to Alyson and pulled the pillow over his head. She *had* been preaching, and she knew it. "Sorry," she said quietly, stepping back and closing the door.

Check the box if you have completed the assignment.

- ❑ I did Days 21–27.
- ❑ I breathed deep the breath of God.
- ❑ I cared for those who care for me.
- ❑ I teamed up with another Christian.
- ❑ I'm working on throwing down my signature sin.
- ❑ I read page 49 (Get Pumped about God's Work).

Coming Attractions

Reality Check 5: Get Pumped About God's Work

Daily Assignments:

- **Read the assigned Bible passages** and answer the questions in the journal.
- **Breathe deep the breath of God** by taking a few deep breaths and praying the Real Deal Prayer: "What do you want to do today, Jesus?" (Action Step 1, p. 6).
- **Care for those who care for you** through acts of kindness (Action Step 4, p. 9).

Assignments for This Week:

- **Team up** with another Christian or three and get real with each other (Action Step 2, p. 7).
- **Throw down your signature sin** by following the six steps that will help you defeat it (Action Step 3, p. 8).
- **Bonus:** Memorize Bible passages that help you live what you say you believe.

Before the End:

- **Start climbing the walls** by starting a relationship with someone who has a different story from yours (Action Step 5, p. 10).

Get Pumped
About God's Work

Days 28&29

SATURDAY/SUNDAY,

Read Ephesians 4:1–7, 11–16.

Date_____

1. According to this passage, what is the purpose of apostles, prophets, evangelists, pastors, and teachers?

2. How have leaders in your church (youth leaders, pastors, Sunday school teachers, etc.) cared for your needs?

3. How might you be able to help "build up" the body of Christ?
- ❑ Bring a few cinder blocks to church with you.
- ❑ Use one of your special talents.
- ❑ Make sure there's plenty of Gatorade.
- ❑ Consistently tithe 10 percent of your income.
- ❑ Ten bucks for every Bible verse memorized!
- ❑ Remember to appreciate and thank those who work for the church.
- ❑ Go to a gym.
- ❑ Support others in their walk with Christ.
- ❑ Other _____.

4. Draw pictures of three people in your church who have cared for your needs, and put their names underneath the pictures.

5. Action Step 4 in this Adventure is to care for those who care for you. This week, try to focus on the people who care for your spiritual growth. What ideas do you have for showing acts of kindness to some of the people you pictured in question 4?

Unanswered ?s:

Get Pumped
About God's Work

Day 30
MONDAY,

Read 1 Thessalonians 5:12-13.   Date_____

1. Paraphrase this passage in exactly eleven words.

2. Fill in the chart below with ways you can respect or disrespect people.

Respect	Disrespect
Listen when people talk to me.	Don't pay attention to people.
Keep my promises.	
	Talk behind people's backs.

3. What can you do to make sure you show respect and gratitude, instead of disrespect, to the leaders of your church?

4. What could you do today for Action Step 4 that would show your gratitude for someone in your church who cares for your spiritual needs?

Unanswered ?s:

Get Pumped
About God's Work

Day 31

TUESDAY,

Read Ephesians 6:18–20.

Date_____

1. What did Paul ask the Ephesians to pray for?

2. In what ways do you think it is hard to be a leader in the church?

3. What ways can you think of to make one of your church leaders' jobs a little easier?
❑ Shine your youth leader's shoes while he or she is giving the lesson.
❑ Listen and be attentive.
❑ Sit in the front row at church and start the wave.
❑ Actually think about the things people are saying.
❑ Applaud every time your Sunday school teacher makes a good point.
❑ Say thank you.
❑ Bring a whole bunch of people to church.
❑ Make suggestions.
❑ Be honest and real.
❑ Other _____.

4. Who is a leader in your church you would like to get to know better? How could you let that person know you would like to spend some time with him or her?

5. Who is one leader in your church you could pray for today? What is it that you could pray for?

Unanswered ?s:

Get Pumped
About God's Work

Day 32

WEDNESDAY,

Read Hebrews 10:19–25.

Date_____

1. According to this passage, why should we encourage one another and meet together regularly?

2. Do you feel you can draw near to God at church? Why or why not? If your answer is no, is there something you could do to help you feel closer to God at church?

3. Who do you think you could help encourage toward love and good deeds? Is this someone you want to put on your list for Action Step 4?

4. If you have "gotten some help" and shared your signature sin with someone, how has that gone? Is this someone you could thank, maybe as part of Action Step 4? If you haven't gotten some help, is there a leader in your church you trust that you could share this with? Maybe he or she could help encourage you toward love and good deeds.

5. Write an encouraging note to someone at church (put your rough draft here). Be sure to use the words *reality*, *cyberspace*, and *hedgehog*.

Unanswered ?s:

Get Pumped About God's Work

Day 33

THURSDAY,

Read Exodus 35:20–29; 36:2–7.

Date_____

1. In your opinion, how would you measure how pumped the men and women in this passage were about God's work? Use the scale below, 1 being not very much, 10 being as much as possible.

| 1 | 2 | 3 | 4 | 5 | 6 | 7 | 8 | 9 | 10 |

2. In your opinion, how pumped about God's work are the people in your church?

| 1 | 2 | 3 | 4 | 5 | 6 | 7 | 8 | 9 | 10 |

3. How pumped about God's work are you?

| 1 | 2 | 3 | 4 | 5 | 6 | 7 | 8 | 9 | 10 |

4. What is something you could give to your church as an offering to support God's work?

❏ A good attitude.
❏ 10% of your allowance.
❏ A special talent.
❏ Volunteer your time.

❏ Your little brother.
❏ Prayer.
❏ Your old beanie babies.
❏ Other _____.

5. How are you doing with throwing down your signature sin? Maybe you are having a hard time with it, or maybe you've given up. Step 6 for Action Step 3 is to start over. You may need to go back and read page 8 again and get a fresh start. You may also want to reevaluate the strategy you developed for Step 4. What do you think you need to do?

Unanswered ?s:

Get Pumped About God's Work

Day 34

FRIDAY,

Read 2 Corinthians 8:1—9.

Date_____

1. If Paul were writing a letter to you and your church today, what would he say about giving and sacrifice?

Paul, an apostle, to the church at _____:

   I thank God that you are _____, except for _____, who's a bit _____.

   Here's what you folks need to do: _____, _____. and _____. And don't forget to _____. (_____, this means you!).

2. Are there any ways you can think of to support and encourage the ministry of your church and leaders besides giving money? How can you go about doing that?

3. Are you ready to promise to "get pumped about God's work" and to care for those who care for you? If yes, make your promise in question 4. If no, would you like to think about it more and decide later? Are there any promises you skipped that you would like to go back to and reconsider?

4. Sign your name and fill in the date below if you're ready to make this promise (or write your own promise). If you decide to make a promise down the road, come back and do this later.

I promise to appreciate and support the work of my church.

Signed: _____ Date: _____

Unanswered ?s:

Get Over the Walls

"Those !%=#+*%s get all the jobs."
"They just want handouts."
"They want to keep us down."
"I don't feel safe around people like that."
"Those !+@=#*%%s are taking over."

Wouldn't you like to think that racism is a thing of the past? Wouldn't it be great if everyone just started accepting people as people, regardless of color or culture? But, just when it seems we might be making progress, you hear comments like those (and you can fill in the !+@=#*%%s yourself).

"Get over it!" you want to scream. "Why can't we all just get along?"

Maybe your generation will finally get rid of racist attitudes, but "getting along" is only half the battle. It will take much longer to break down the walls.

You see, racism has a one-two punch. First, it's the attitude—the hatred, the mistrust. But, second, there are the sharp divisions these feelings have created in our society. Different races live in different places, go to different schools and churches, do different things. We've built walls. Even if we cure the attitudes, we'll still have the walls.

Consider the white Christian who says, "I love black people; I just don't know any." Maybe that's your situation, too, whatever your race. If your normal patterns of life don't bring you into contact with people of other cultures, what can you do?

Change your patterns of life. Seriously, get over one of those walls. Find a way to connect with someone of another culture. That's the only way we're going to overcome the centuries of division.

Not all the walls are racial. You may be isolated from, say, people of other faiths, or people with disabilities. You may need to make an effort to climb one of those walls.

Why is this important? Because it's trendy? Because it fits someone's political agenda? No. Because it's what Jesus did and what he wants to do through you. "For he himself is our peace, who has made the two one and has destroyed the barrier, the dividing wall of hostility" (Ephesians 2:14, NIV). That verse is talking about Jews and Gentiles, the major wall in Jesus' culture, but we can find other examples in the way Jesus dealt with women, Samaritans, lepers, and prostitutes. Jesus was a wall-breaker, and he asks us to follow him.

So if you're still nursing hateful attitudes toward people who aren't like you, get over it! And if your attitude's fine, but you still find a wall dividing you from others, get yourself over that wall!

Alyson and Jen were probably the only ones arguing theology in the lunchroom.

"But Jesus was human, too," Alyson said.

"Yes, but he never sinned."

"Well, we know that now. But at the time—I mean, in order for the temptations to be . . . well, *tempting*, there had to be the *possibility*—"

"Mind if we join you?" It was two friends, Barb and Chanteel.

"What are you two all excited about?" Barb asked.

"Mmm, nothing important," Jen replied.

"Sure sounded important," Barb said. "Probably some guy."

"That's it," Jen answered. And they *had* been talking about Brian earlier. She was holding her ground sexually, but she felt Brian slipping away. She felt very shaky about this, which was why she asked Alyson about temptation. But she certainly wasn't ready to share her struggle with anyone else.

"Figures," Barb teased. "Who is it?"

"Well, actually," Alyson smiled, "we were talking about Jesus."

"Jesus!" Barb exploded. "I didn't know you knew anything about Jesus."

"You never asked," answered Alyson cautiously.

Chanteel caught Alyson's eye across the table and said quietly. "I know Jesus, too."

"Really? That's great," Alyson replied. "I can't believe we've known each other all this time and I never knew you were a Christian."

"I guess you never asked," Chanteel said quietly.

"Which is no surprise to me," Barb announced. "There are all sorts of things about black folks you never asked."

Alyson was startled. She went through life rather colorblind, and she was proud of that. Barb and Chanteel weren't "her African-American friends," they were just friends. Was she now being accused of prejudice?

Barb went on, "It's like your life is over there, and our life is over here. You know what I'm saying? Have you ever been over to Chanteel's house?"

"Well, no."

"And you haven't been to mine. You ever invited her to your house?

"No, but you haven't invited—"

"I know, I know, but that's the thing. It's a line no one will cross."

There was silence for a moment. Their minds raced—accusing, defending, apologizing, excusing.

"Cross," repeated Jen. The others looked at her. "We were talking about Jesus, and you said there's a line we don't *cross*. That's all."

Chanteel looked at Alyson with gentle brown eyes. "Would you like to come to my church sometime?"

The bell rang, a high-pitched hoot that set the room in motion. The four girls remained still as Alyson considered this invitation. For a second she saw in Chanteel's eyes the eyes of Jesus, beckoning. "Yes, I would," she said.

"When?"

Check the box if you have completed the assignment.

❑ I did Days 28–34.
❑ I breathed deep the breath of God.
❑ I cared for those who care for me.
❑ I teamed up with another Christian.
❑ I'm working on throwing down my signature sin.
❑ I read page 58 (Get Over the Walls).

Coming Attractions

Reality Check 6: Get Over the Walls

Daily Assignments:

- **Read the assigned Bible passages** and answer the questions in the journal.
- **Breathe deep the breath of God** by a taking a few deep breaths and praying the Real Deal Prayer: "What do you want to do today, Jesus?" (Action Step 1, p. 6).
- **Care for those who care for you** through acts of kindness (Action Step 4, p. 9).

Assignments for This Week:

- **Team up** with another Christian or three and get real with each other (Action Step 2, p. 7).
- **Throw down your signature sin** by following the six steps that will help you defeat it (Action Step 3, p. 8).
- **Bonus:** Memorize Bible passages that help you live what you say you believe.

Before the End:

- **Start climbing the walls** by starting a relationship with someone who has a different story from yours (Action Step 5, p. 10).

Get Over the Walls

Days 35&36

SATURDAY/SUNDAY,

Read Luke 10:25–37.

Date_____

1. If this were a modern-day story on *20/20*, how would they report it?

2. As you can see in this passage, there was prejudice against the Samaritans in Jesus' time. What groups of people do you think experience racism or prejudice today?

3. What groups of people do you have racist or prejudiced ideas about? (If you can't think of any group, think harder.) How or why do you think those ideas got there?

4. What do you think Jesus would do or say today about racism or prejudice in our society? Who do you think he would be spending his time with?

5. Action Step 5 in this Adventure is to start climbing the walls of prejudice and racism. Just like for Action Step 3, the first step is to admit you have a problem. Try finishing this statement: I am prejudiced against _____

_____ .

Unanswered ?s:

Get Over the Walls

Day 37
Monday,

Read Mark 1:40—42.

Date_____

1. How did Jesus treat this leper who had been shunned and considered untouchable by society?

2. Who in today's world would be a group of people shunned similarly to the lepers of Jesus' day? What is your feeling about that?

3. You may feel you are not prejudiced or racist. And if that's true, great. But it may also be that you just don't get out of your cultural circle much. Finish this sentence by checking the boxes: In the course of an average month, I have meaningful contact with

❏ African-Americans.   ❏ Poor people.
❏ Hispanics.   ❏ Rich people.
❏ Caucasians.   ❏ Jocks.
❏ Asians.   ❏ Drug addicts.
❏ Native Americans.   ❏ Computer wizzes.
❏ Homosexuals.   ❏ Popular people.
❏ Elderly people.   ❏ Unpopular people.
❏ Women.   ❏ Overweight people.
❏ Men.   ❏ People with disabilities.

If you're honest about it, you can probably add more groups than we can—so go ahead.

4. What are your plans for Action Step 5? Did question 3 give you any ideas for someone you could get to know?

Unanswered ?s:

Get Over the Walls

Day 38
TUESDAY,

Read John 4:1–42.

Date_____

1. If you were to cast a movie that was based on this passage, what race would Jesus be, and what type of person would he meet? Why did you make these choices?

2. In this passage Jesus "astonished" the disciples by talking to a woman. In what ways is there prejudice against women today? Do you feel you have a prejudice against women (or men)? What could you do to climb that wall?

3. How does it seem Jesus treated people he came in contact with?

❑ He treated them with compassion.
❑ He acted as if he knew it all.
❑ He touched them, but then he washed with antibacterial soap.
❑ He looked down on them.
❑ He treated everyone equally.
❑ He avoided them.

❑ He scolded them for not flossing.
❑ He just used them to make a point.
❑ He loved them.
❑ He cared for their needs.
❑ He broke down all the walls.
❑ He only came in contact with a certain kind of person.

4. How do you treat people who are different from you? What are you good at? What do you need to work on?

5. How are you doing with throwing down your signature sin? Maybe you are having a hard time with it, or maybe you've given up. Step 6 for Action Step 3 is to start over. You may need to go back and read page 8 again and get a fresh start. You may also want to reevaluate the strategy you developed for Step 4. What do you think you need to do?

Unanswered ?s:

Get Over the Walls

Day 39
WEDNESDAY,

Read Mark 9:33–41.

Date_____

1. What did Jesus say one must do in order to be the first?

2. With this passage in mind, what do you think Jesus would say about the denominational divisions in the church today? What about the cultural and racial divisions in the church today?

3. If Jesus commanded you to give a cup of water in his name to someone who is not "one of your group," who do you think that someone would be?

4. What can you do to be more of a servant to people who are different from you? What is one specific way you can do that?

5. How have you been doing with the promises you've made during this Adventure? If there are promises you wanted to think about a little more, have you come to any decisions? If you are ready to make any of the promises that you wanted to come back to, now would be a good time to do that.

Unanswered ?s:

Get Over the Walls

Day 40
THURSDAY,

Read Matthew 25:31–46.

Date_____

1. How often in the course of a month do you come in meaningful contact with any of the following:

❑ The hungry?
❑ The thirsty?
❑ Strangers?

❑ Those who need clothes?
❑ The sick?
❑ Those in prison?

2. How often do you come in contact with the above people and just walk right by? How do you tend to feel when you see such people?

3. How can you take care of the needs of the hungry, the thirsty, strangers, those who need clothes, the sick, and those in prison if you never have any meaningful contact with them? (Sorry, rhetorical question.) The real question is: What can you do to make sure you are coming into meaningful contact with some of these people?

4. What is one meaningful thing you can do to serve one of these people? How will you go about that?

5. How are you doing with the other action steps (breathe deep the breath of God, team up, throw down your signature sin, and care for those who care for you)? If you haven't been following too closely, why not start fresh today?

Unanswered ?s:

Get Over the Walls

Day 41
FRIDAY,

Read Psalm 19:12–14.

Date_____

1. The psalmist asks forgiveness for "hidden faults." As you've thought about the walls in your life, have any previously "hidden faults" come to light? If so, what?

2. With that in mind, rewrite these verses, specifically zeroing in on the walls you want to get over.

3. How are your plans going for Action Step 5 (start climbing the walls)? Is there something more you need to do or plan for this action step?

4. Are you ready to promise to "get over the walls" and to "start climbing the walls"? If yes, make your promise in question 5. If no, would you like to think about it more and decide later? Are there any promises you skipped that you would like to go back to and reconsider?

5. Sign your name and fill in the date below if you're ready to make this promise (or write your own promise). If you decide to make a promise down the road, come back and do this later.

I promise to identify and deal with my prejudices.

Signed: _____ Date: _____

Unanswered ?s:

Get a Job

W here do you want to go today?"
In its rush toward world domination, Microsoft paused briefly and gave us a wonderful advertising line.

"Where do you want to go today?"

The sound and pictures of their commercials make you feel that anything anywhere is literally at your fingertips. Just tap a few keys, and your computer will get you there.

"Where do you want to go today?"

The world is smaller than ever, thanks to technology. You can chat nightly with people across the globe, read a newspaper from another hemisphere, or do research in a library an ocean away.

But Christians have been pulling the world together for centuries. Missionaries have gone to the farthest reaches of the planet, not with machines but with a message: *The Creator is dying to know you.* Stone Age headhunters in Ecuador, New Age skiers in Switzerland, and underage gang members in Los Angeles have all heard the word and given their lives to Christ. What in the world is God doing? Plenty.

You can be a part of that. When you take a good look at what's most important in life, you *have* to be a part of that. All right, get a business degree and your company could send you to China to find better ways to sell, say, Mountain Dew to those billions of people. Or, become a missionary and find better ways to introduce billions of Chinese to Jesus Christ. *Hmmmm.* Which one makes the world a better place? You decide.

We're not saying you *have* to be a missionary or a pastor. You can serve God in a lot of different careers. You don't have to be a full-time missionary, you don't have to travel across the world, but whatever you do, wherever you go, start planning now to serve God with your life. Before he ascended to heaven, Jesus told his disciples, "You will receive power when the Holy Spirit comes on you; and you will be my witnesses in Jerusalem, and in all Judea and Samaria, and to the ends of the earth" (Acts 1:8). Near or far, Christians *will be* witnesses of God's power in their life.

"Where do you want to go today?" Where does God want you to go? It's never too soon to start asking.

M ike trudged through the streets of town. Cars passed, some filled with noisy teenagers, but he turned away, not wanting to be recognized.

It was late Friday night, and Mike had just watched his basketball team win a close game. He had a great seat, too, right at the end of the bench. One nod from the coach, and he'd have been in there, running, jumping, passing, shooting, diving for loose balls. He never got the nod.

So, while his teammates stripped off their sweaty uniforms, Mike quietly changed out of his dry one. They hooted and hollered in the shower while Mike grabbed his gym bag and started the long walk home. He could have waited around to catch a ride. But walking would give him time to think.

"What's really important to you, Mike?" He could hear Alyson's voice in his head. She was really annoying lately, pushing him to be more disciplined, more focused, more Christian. At least she cared. . . .

"What's really important to me?" he asked out loud as he walked. "Well, basketball." B-ball had been the love of Mike's life since he was seven, when his dad put up a backboard beside their driveway. But was he important to basketball?

"What else is important to me?" he wondered, crossing the street. "Girls." But here there was heartache, too. They all wanted to be "just friends." For a year he had a crush on Alyson's best friend, Jen. When she finally broke up with that loser Brian, Mike made a play for her. But no, she "wasn't ready" for another relationship.

"Look at your future," his guidance counselor said. "What do you see yourself becoming? What career would you like to go into?"

Something involving basketball and girls, he thought. Great; I'll be a professional male cheerleader. Do they have those?

"I have no life," he said out loud, crossing the parking lot of the boarded-up K-mart. So what were his options? His sister would tell him to get serious about Jesus, to breathe deep the breath *of God.* Seemed a little much to Mike. But he had to admit something dramatic was happening with Alyson. Still, he didn't want to enter Alyson's Wonderland. He needed to carve out a life for himself.

Mike stopped in front of his church. He didn't remember deciding to walk that way. Wandering around to the back, out of sight of passing cars, he knelt in the cool grass outside his Sunday school room.

"God, I don't wanna go all wacky like my sister," he said. "But you gotta help me. My life right now really—" Mike saw a paper airplane in the shrubs, one of several he remembered throwing around the room last Sunday. He unfolded the plane.

TUTORS NEEDED the flier said. The church took a van to an inner-city ministry after school every day. *Hmmmm.* Mike had always been pretty good with math and science; maybe he could help some kids. For the first time in a long time, he felt genuinely excited.

Wait! he thought. *It's after school. I'll miss basketball practice. Right. Big deal!*

Check the box if you have completed the assignment.

- ❑ I did Days 35–41.
- ❑ I breathed deep the breath of God.
- ❑ I cared for those who care for me.
- ❑ I teamed up with another Christian.
- ❑ I'm working on throwing down my signature sin.
- ❑ I'm starting to climb the walls.
- ❑ I read page 67 (Get a Job).

Coming Attractions

Reality Check 7: Get a Job   **Reality Check 8:** Get a Life

Daily Assignments:

- **Read the assigned Bible passages** and answer the questions in the journal.
- **Breathe deep the breath of God** by taking a few deep breaths and praying the Real Deal Prayer: "What do you want to do today, Jesus?" (Action Step 1, p. 6).
- **Care for those who care for you** through acts of kindness (Action Step 4, p. 9).

Assignments for This Week:

- **Read page 75** (Get a Life).
- **Team up** with another Christian or three and get real with each other (Action Step 2, p. 7).
- **Throw down your signature sin** by following the six steps that will help you defeat it (Action Step 3, p. 8).
- **Bonus:** Memorize Bible passages that help you live what you say you believe.

Before the End:

- **Start climbing the walls** by starting a relationship with someone who has a different story from yours (Action Step 5, p. 10).

Get a Job

Read Matthew 28:16–20; Mark 12:28–31.

Date_____

1. How are these two passages similar, and how are they different?

Similar	Different

2. How many different ways can you think of to love your neighbor as yourself in ten seconds? List them here.

3. Who are your neighbors?
- ❏ Nice people.
- ❏ Your parents.
- ❏ Good-looking people.
- ❏ Drug addicts.
- ❏ People who love you.
- ❏ Popular kids at school.
- ❏ People with a lot of pierced body parts.
- ❏ Prisoners.
- ❏ Homosexuals.
- ❏ Your church leaders.
- ❏ People with money.
- ❏ Your friends.
- ❏ African-Americans.
- ❏ Native Americans.
- ❏ Asians.
- ❏ Hispanics.
- ❏ Caucasians.

4. According to these two Bible passages, what is your job?

Unanswered ?s:

Get a Job

DAY 44

Day 44

MONDAY,

Read Acts 8:26–35.

Date_____

1. What was Philip's job in this passage?

2. You're Philip. The angel gives you these instructions. What do you say?

3. Is there a specific "job" (or two or three) you think God is calling you to? Explain.

4. What can you do to make sure you are sensitive to the leadings of God and follow the "jobs" he has set out for you?

5. Have you ever felt called to be any of the following:

❏ A parent.

    ❏ A missionary.

❏ A teacher.

    ❏ A pastor.

❏ An artist.

    ❏ A youth worker.

❏ A scientist.

    ❏ An evangelist.

6. What could you do and who could you talk with to get more information about a "job" you listed in question 3 or 5?

Unanswered ?s:

Get a Job

Day 45
TUESDAY,

Read Matthew 5:13–16.

Date_____

1. What does this passage say "you are"?

2. What are some ways you can be these things in your world?

3. If the world's light depended on how much you let your light shine, how bright do you think the world would be?

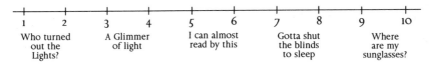

1	2	3	4	5	6	7	8	9	10
Who turned out the Lights?		A Glimmer of light		I can almost read by this		Gotta shut the blinds to sleep		Where are my sunglasses?	

4. What would you have to do to let your light shine more brightly in your world? How could you go about doing that?

Unanswered ?s:

Get a Job

Day 46
WEDNESDAY,

Read Matthew 9:35–38.

Date_____

1. Who are the workers Jesus is talking about in this passage?

2. What is the harvest Jesus is talking about?

3. You are one of these workers. How good a job do you think you are doing?

4. How do you think you can do this "job" best?

❑ Hit the streets with my Bible.
❑ Talk to my friends more about my life with God.
❑ Be more open to opportunities God brings to me.
❑ Wear Christian T-shirts.
❑ Invite friends to church and youth group.
❑ Become a missionary.
❑ Set up a pulpit in the middle of school and start preaching.
❑ Live my life as an example.
❑ Tell people they're going to hell.

Unanswered ?s:

Get a Job

Day 47
THURSDAY,

Read 2 Corinthians 5:14–21.

Date_____

1. According to this passage, why should we be excited to share the good news about Jesus?

2. What difference would it make in your life if you stopped evaluating people by what the world thinks of them and started viewing them from an eternal perspective?

Worldly	Eternal

3. Is there someone you know whom you could share the good news about Jesus with? How best could you do that? (There are many different ways to evangelize; each person must find a way that fits who he or she is.)

4. Are you ready to promise to "get a job"? If yes, make your promise in question 5. If no, would you like to think about it more and decide later? Are there any promises you skipped that you would like to go back to and reconsider?

5. Sign your name and fill in the date below if you're ready to make this promise (or write your own promise). If you decide to make a promise down the road, come back and do this later.

I promise to join God in his work in this world.

Signed: _____ Date: _____

Unanswered ?s:

Get a Life

People can make a big deal over the stupidest things—why don't they get a life? The teacher who hasn't cracked a smile since the Reagan Administration but insists you spit out your gum. The computer wiz who's all worked up about his latest Java script. The groupie who has every square inch of her room papered with posters of the group *du jour*. The guy who can recite every *Seinfeld* episode by heart and does so regularly.

Get a life! There must be more important things to think about. What's really important? Your school's star basketball player spends hours on the court refining his game, hoping for a scholarship to a Division I school. Your valedictorian candidates write extra papers to outdo one another for that honor. Some of your classmates are already making their life plans—business careers with six-figure salaries; med school and a private practice; Hollywood stardom. We don't roll our eyes when these people talk about what's most important to them, but maybe they need to get a life, too.

When all is said and done, money, success, and stardom won't matter. Jesus matters.

There's nothing wrong with getting good grades, excelling at extracurricular activities, or having big plans. But it's even more important to live each day in the power and love of Jesus. That's the "life" you want to "get."

"Life itself was in him," says John about the Word, Jesus Christ (John 1:4). And God proved it by raising Jesus from the dead. There was no way the author of life could stay dead (Acts 3:15). The Bible goes on to promise amazing power to us. "The Spirit of God, who raised Jesus from the dead, lives in you. And just as he raised Christ from the dead, he will give life to your mortal body by this same Spirit living within you" (Romans 8:11). We can share in Christ's resurrection life!

Paul prayed that the Ephesian Christians would know "his incomparably great power for us who believe. That power is like the working of his mighty strength, which he exerted in Christ when he raised him from the dead" (Ephesians 3:19–20, NIV).

The resurrection of Jesus is not just a nice story to tell at Easter, it's a living reality for us. It's the source of our life and power. It changes everything for us. We can take risks for the Lord, knowing his awesome power is backing us up. We can have confidence when we face temptation. And we don't have to adopt the priorities of everyone around us, because we *have* a life, a life where Jesus Christ is more important than anything else.

"Since you have been raised to a new life with Christ, set your sights on the realities of heaven," the Bible says, "where Christ sits at God's right hand in the place of honor and power" (Colossians 3:1–2).

Grab your life today. Live in the power of Jesus' resurrection.

Get a Life

Day 48

FRIDAY,

Read 2 Corinthians 4:7–18.

Date_____

1. Paraphrase this passage in a way that makes more sense to you (and just for kicks, don't use the letter G).

2. What does it mean to fix your eyes not on what is seen, but on what is unseen (NIV)?

Seen	Unseen

3. In what way has knowing Jesus changed your life?

4. In what ways would you like Jesus to change your life more?

5. Action Step 1 in this Adventure has been about paying more attention to God. What has been your experience with this action step throughout the last 48 days?

Unanswered ?s:

Get a Life

Day 49
SATURDAY,

Read Philippians 3:10–16.

Date_____

1. What is behind that you would like to forget? What would you like to look forward to ahead? Use the picture of the road to write your answer.

Behind

Ahead

2. What is the "prize" mentioned in this passage? What steps have you taken during this Adventure that you would like to continue in order to press on toward that prize?

3. How are you doing with throwing down your signature sin? Maybe you are having a hard time with it, or maybe you've given up. Step 6 for Action Step 3 is to start over. You may need to go back and read page 8 again and get a fresh start. You may also want to reevaluate the strategy you developed for Step 4. What do you think you need to do?

4. No one is saying you can throw down your signature sin in only 50 days. For many it is a lifelong struggle. But don't get discouraged, because the power of Christ and his resurrection are working for you. If you've done well, congratulations, and keep it up. If you've had a hard time of it, don't give up, and keep trying.

Unanswered ?s:

Get a Life

Day 50
SUNDAY,

Read Luke 24:1–12.

Date_____

1. Which characters in this passage would you have acted most like?

❑ The women   ❑ The apostles   ❑ Peter

2. What does this passage say about God's promises?

3. How have the action steps been for you? Are there any action steps you would like to continue after this Adventure is over? Or is there one you would like to pursue a little deeper?

4. Are you ready to promise to "get a life"? If yes, make your promise in question 5. If no, would you like to think about it more and decide later? Are there any promises you skipped that you would like to promise before this Adventure is over?

❑ I promise to spend some time each day with God.
❑ I promise to be honest and make friendships really count.
❑ I promise to live a life that pleases God.
❑ I promise to make family relationships a priority.
❑ I promise to appreciate and support the work of my church.
❑ I promise to identify and deal with my prejudices.
❑ I promise to join God in his work in this world.

Signed: _____ Date: _____

5. Sign your name and fill in the date below if you're ready to make this promise (or write your own promise). If you decide to make a promise down the road, come back and do this later.

I promise to live my life one day at a time through the power of Christ.

Signed: _____ Date: _____

Unanswered ?s:

Final Backcheck

Check the box if you have completed the assignment.

❑ I did most of Days 1–50.
❑ I breathed deep the breath of God.
❑ I teamed up.
❑ I've begun to face up to my signature sin.
❑ I cared for those who care for me.
❑ I started to climb the walls.
❑ I memorized Bible passages that help me live what I say I believe.

Tell Us Your Story

We've been praying that this Adventure would make a difference in your life. And we would love to hear your story. As you're finishing up this Adventure, we're already hard at work on a new one. But the Adventure is for you. So send us your story. We'd love to hear from you. Or send an e-mail with your comments to:

T50DSA@aol.com

**Mainstay Church
Resources
Editorial Department
P.O. Box 30
Wheaton, IL 60189**

The Real Deal 50-Day Spiritual Adventure

	Price	Qty	Total
2920 The Real Deal Student Journal	$7.00	_____	_____
7846 The Real Deal Scripture Pack	$2.00	_____	_____
		Subtotal	_____

Power Up 50-Day Spiritual Adventure

	Price	Qty	Total
2820 Power Up Student Journal	$6.00	_____	_____
1866 When the Troops Are Tired Guidebook	$6.00	_____	_____
		Subtotal	_____

In the House 50-Day Spiritual Adventure

	Price	Qty	Total
2720 In the House Student Journal	$6.00	_____	_____
1809 I Like Church, But . . . Guidebook	$6.00	_____	_____
		Subtotal	_____

I'm So Confused 50-Day Spiritual Adventure

	Price	Qty	Total
2620 I'm So Confused Student Journal	$6.00	_____	_____
1761 When Life Becomes a Maze Guidebook	$6.00	_____	_____
		Subtotal	_____
		TOTAL	_____

Add 10% for UPS shipping/handling ($4.00 minimum)	_____
Canadian or Illinois residents add 7% GST/sales tax	_____
TOTAL AMOUNT ENCLOSED	_____

Please fill out the information below:

Your name _____

Address* _____

State/Prov _____ Zip/Code _____ Phone _____

I'd like to pay by: ❏ Check ❏ Money Order ❏ VISA ❏ MasterCard ❏ Discover

*Note: UPS will not deliver to a P.O. Box.

Copy this form and send it with your check to Mainstay Church Resources, Box 30 Wheaton, IL 60189. In Canada: The Chapel Ministries, Box 2000, Waterdown, ON L0R 2H0. Or call 1-800-224-2735 (in Canada 1-800-461-4114) for credit card orders.

M089SG